Praise for *milk tongue*

"Successive poetry collections do not follow popular logic regarding successive children. One does not become more relaxed about what they are birthing. If anything, the stakes of possibility increase. Mathieu's *milk tongue* is an appropriately ambitious collection that burns a path across a land it loves, a land it is making as much as it is reclaiming. The fire in the phrasing. The formal denaturing of poem and page. '[T]he thick mess of us' that is shown to be both scientific and carnal. '[I]t's hard work remembering to be human,' but this collection has a strong motor, applying a lyric force that takes us the distance."

—Kyle Dargan, author of *PANZER HERZ: A Live Dissection*

"Within the first two hundred words of Toni Morrison's *A Mercy*, Florens notes: 'One question is who is responsible. Another is can you read?' For me, these are the questions—of deep reckoning and attention—that flower in the fields of milk tongue's pages. Irène Mathieu reads her worlds keenly, spaciously, making a work alive with power and rippled with mystery. She summons what feels like a geological wisdom. River, leaves, perception, milk in the mouth of a descendant (also Mathieu) effortfully attuning herself to lineages of being and sound: 'clutch of clay: everything is made of something. / I lay my language on it and then I take that away / and put down something that comes before / language.'"

—Aracelis Girmay, author of *The Black Maria*

"Though the poems of *milk tongue* reckon with the given world, Irène Mathieu claims allegiance not to what's allegedly true about it, but to what she has come to know as true through her experience as a daughter, lover, mother, neighbor, and caregiver. Each poem documents 'the aftershocks of becoming/oscillating   in the dark century,' their lines riding the rhythms of embodied knowledge, sleepless nights, 'hynagogic conjure,' and feminine folkways, all somatic or sidereal epistemologies that both register and resist our nation's violent and inequitable systems. Mathieu's Black feminist poetics powerfully reminds us: 'A witch is someone who turns anger into light.'"

—Brian Teare, author of *Doomstead Days*

milk tongue

milk tongue

POEMS

Irène Mathieu

Deep Vellum

Dallas, TX

Deep Vellum Publishing
3000 Commerce St., Dallas, Texas 75226
deepvellum.org · @deepvellum

Deep Vellum is a 501c3 nonprofit literary arts organization
founded in 2013 with the mission to bring
the world into conversation through literature.

Support for this publication has been provided in part by the National
Endowment for the Arts, the Texas Commission on the Arts, the City of Dallas
Office of Arts and Culture, and the George and Fay Young Foundation.

Paperback ISBN: 9781646052660
eBook ISBN: 9781646052875

Library Of Congress Control Number: 2023003946

Cover art by Ginger Huebner
Cover design and typesetting by
David Wojciechowski | www.davidwojo.com

Printed in the United States of America

for JGR, and the promises we made

CONTENTS

iii. yellow is the color of my wanting

iv. I am not absent, as never before –

the flights of this journey
mapless   uncertain
and necessary as water.

– Audre Lorde

i. turns anger into light

After emailing a copy of Audre Lorde's essay
"The Uses of the Erotic" to a friend

because of what we said at dinner about how
our bodies feel to us. To spell it out,
this is after salting my new yoga mat, which
my teacher swears will help with the slipping,
after walking the dog through piles of melting
slush – December rain on snow on mud –
after skimming an article that suggested our
phones are becoming extensions of our minds,
or something to that effect, while contemplating
all the powers I don't know I'm giving up
this week, as measured in the light-years
between my language and my body.
Last week, my partner said, when I was falling
asleep I murmured *witchcraft witchcraft witchcraft*
into the pillow – hypnagogic conjure I must have
inherited somewhere in the last millennium.
You know, I say, holding leaves inside my cheek,
this used to be illegal – meaning the chlorophyll
leaching directly into my bloodstream.
I worry how the screen gathers my energy,
renders my melatonin adrift & inert.
It won't stop raining this decade, and we did it
with our unfeeling bodies. Eventually,
while falling asleep
I try to fall back a few centuries, sifting through
piles all the women like us left behind – *craft*
is an exercise in making, a skill that wants practice,
i.e., to become rippled with gold through every
fascial plane, and also completely soluble across
space-time – don't pretend it makes sense
when I put it like that.
Instead, take the broad leaf, the wax,

the unrolled cloth, mouthful of river, quartz,
clutch of clay: everything is made of something.
I lay my language on it and then I take that away
and put down something that comes before
language. I put down something that comes
before   I put down something and
I come before   I put down before
language   something that comes

My head is full of powers

Recently I cut eight inches of my hair and counted six grays.

My mother's hair once was the color of dark copper.

Someone said, you should have donated your hair.

My parents' dog once had hair the color of raven, but she's full of grays now.

I think each gray hair I grow has special powers.

Once a month my mother dyes her hair with henna the color of burnt chestnut.

My parents' dog is full of special powers.

My mother used to have short hair, but recently it's grown long.

In pictures with her father, taken before I was born, the waves on their heads glint redly.

There is a reason we associate red with anger.

My parents' dog can hear things no one else can, not even her brother.

My mother talks about some things she has heard, and not about others.

The reason is that anger is hot enough to burn you up.

My fourth decade as a human, as far as I know, has already begun.

Gray seems a witchy color.

I can't tell you how old my mother is, or she will hear me and grow angry.

Witchy as thundercloud, as pebble, as sea foam, as amniotic fluid.

My parents' dog senses what gathers in the woods beyond her ears.

My hair gathered in the trash can while my head lightened.

My mother has been able to teach me certain things without saying them.

That is, no one else can hear some things she has said.

Hot as lava, as chili pepper, as solar flare, as strawberry poison-dart frog.

I should have donated my special powers.

It's never too late to reveal certain things, even after many dog-years or ghost-years.

Someone said, do you try to write political poems

The answer is that I write redly.

My parents' dog and my mother bark only when necessary.

I hear them deepening, full of gray.

Everything on my head is in my head.

I learned it from my mother.

A witch is someone who turns anger into light.

the forest fire of family trees

the problem is we don't know
that many ways of doing things
for instance, neither of us can
fry an egg without public radio
chattering in our ears, & there
are worse blueprints for a home,
like what my grandfather taught
my uncle. we think we know
people until we see the way
they eat a banana, totally unlike
how we peel and devour the fruit,
only instead of eating a banana
it's something way bigger,
like loving another person.
as the snowflakes get thicker
I hear myself say exactly
what my mother would say
when faced with this same
situation, and I say it
in her voice. it's not that I'm
ashamed to share all my DNA
and most of my life with these
two people, it's just that I worry.
it's not easy to recognize
the odor of toxins you
release, day after day,
which, when rearranged,
spells door. you cross
the threshold & think it's just
the cologne of the world,
not the smoke in your
blood, not grass burning
from the little fires ignited
by your feet.

fourteenth attempt at going home

in the cities of the dead, trumpets flare.
this is a second line for alluvial plains, but
the Lyft driver believes the climate's been getting
one degree warmer every year basically forever.
I want to know who put this trash in my city.
closure is being certain there is nothing to resurrect,
which is maybe an unholy realization to have
on Easter, but it would be worse if I lied to you.
the night before, I took myself out, I ordered the
fanciest cocktail, I mopped up the roux in my bowl
with French bread. drunk tourists are my least
favorite kind. I remember my nights
full of rum on an island, the feeling
of land slipping away. the Superdome
should be a national monument because the
air jammed in my throat the first moment I
saw it. if you picture people trying to sleep all
lined up like that, it makes you think of something
else. I remember my mother telling me how
graveyards are constructed here, every
body in an aboveground box, so water won't
loosen the bones and worry them out of the loam.
I've seen it more than once now, plus a lone
motorcycle weaving around the tombs.
how does it feel to be a ruinous topography.
if you don't believe me when I tell you where
I'm from I'll give you one star. no, I'll give you
an unlit sky, no illuminated guide. I can't stop
writing about a place that no longer exists,
whose light I still use for navigation. after every crescent
city parade there's a flock of crêpe paper seagulls
trying to escape gravity, and I can imagine worse
miracles to tell my future selves.

lullaby

scrape a baby's white tongue
and if chunks crumble off, it's milk.
if the tongue bleeds, it's thrush.

let the baby thrash, looking for food.
if I find a wellspring, let me drink.
this is called responsive parenting.

don't rush to console me – let the baby
cry.   this is sleep training.
let me palm the dark edges of my
own vision when the light goes out,
let me taste what grows in my mouth.

follow the little spine to where it ends
in a feathered tail   whipping in a bone straw
innervating my wrists. I can tell myself

reach for this, or *grab that* and it is done.
I smell food   I drink, my thrum a
tired anthem. I cannot tell from here
if my tongue is overgrown
or simply overfed.

the room is full of shuddering.
milk tongue, milk tongue, your song's
getting sour. I haven't slept well
since I was born.

as a bird, thrush doesn't so much sing
as insist.   *look, blood!*
the baby assumes that everything in the room
has an explanation:
milk, here   blood, there   and why.

if a baby is sick, take blood from the wrist.
ask it why. I'll never be nursed this way
again. my mother says when I cried
my father always came running.
this explains the color of my feathers.

it's hard to tell if the baby's getting
bigger or if the room is shrinking, but
something's arise
symbiotically this species trills a warbling ballad.

when a thrush lands on the windowsill
tell the baby   *even birds drink milk.*
I can't tell what's inside the room and
what's out. I'd give up blood to know.

the baby's cried too long again.
I'll turn out the light, place her face-up.
hush the rooting mouth still in training –
I won't ask questions of my tongue.

aubade with atony

It's happened again.

I've dozed myself into the
straightjacket of
a s l e e p - b u t - a w a k e ,
mummified   to   silence,
breath   snatched   in   my
throat.

sleep paralysis is not quite
a   haunting,
nor   is   it   like   receiving
messages from
a god who doesn't want to
claim you

– it's an opposite day
                         at night
in broad   daylight,
open-mouthed   in mind
only   –
         from my bedroom
doorway
I'm just a body slowly rising
&   falling –   from the
outside: natural.

I won't compare it to the
magician's assistant –
her vision, moments before
she was sawed   in two
that first time they ran the
box trick   backstage:
unfortunate blood seeping

between pine boards,
her face screwed up in
perpetual surprise
like the springs of a stopped
clock clawing   in its case.

I'm   spooked   by   the
knowledge that anything
could come into me at a
time like this
and I would not be able to
scream.

I hinge, teeter blankly –

what energies wait at the
edges
of my arteries to jump into
their slowing stream,
what bright panic leaps like
static from me   –
even my lover, casually
curling beside   feels
        like a fire.
the world has
        inverted
& from the outside it looks
        natural.

this isn't like the dawns I
nearly inherited
of   women   half-awake
beside men fully asleep,

nightmarishly walking this
way for lifetimes,   women
who
thought   the box   would
give
way   –   escape hatch
open
them into   intact   on
other
         sides,   like magic.

that my sister stares, wide-
mouthed, when I tell her
what I feel some days
between states of sleep /
wake
(it happens to her, too)
doesn't mean

we've inherited the same
lacquered box
covered with men on
horseback wielding spears,
which   sat   on   my
grandmother's dining room
table
for half a century, doesn't
mean we'll be trapped
inside
a box (like Pandora reaching
into a Venus flytrap
in some other version of the
myth),
or quartered, or clipped.

I don't have to open the box
to know what's inside.
just knowing that I could,
even if the box is out of
sight,
charred in the   pit of a
landfill,   is the same as

fear's slippery wrist pinning
me to the ground,
trying to own my name.

what we call sanity is just an empty road through the mountains

the distance between what I thought I saw
and the knowing that I didn't

is the distance between here and a seedy motel –
the one lane lined with roadkill – –

and in the time it takes to journey from rupture
to diagnosis

you can get there. an old woman will be at the desk
in the lobby. ignore the color of the carpet,
the dank wallpaper. tell her you want room 309.

then sleep.   sleep.

haibun in the place of sleep

for Jeannette

these soft organs slip around each other on the couch.   my ankles ashy.
when did I last call my grandma?   hair half undone.   all the people I
miss   crowd around my ears   like the colored beads I used to collect
as a child.   they weighed down my pockets;   they weigh down my
eyelids. what to do with my belly at this hour.

when I am too tired I

don't finish.

I shouldn't say too much right now.   all the deaths fly into my arms
with tissue-paper wings / with wire legs.   I remember each like
dried salt drops   how the ocean ghosts my epidermis   one day
someone sits you down and says,   here is the container for eyes,   here
is the one for lungs. on the couch I sort I sort,   restless   my throat spins
itself to a strand   –   nearly snaps.

hair forest of my forearm,   let your animals rest.   the floor lamp burns
letters into my forehead. I'm too tired to walk to the mirror. little curls
spoon the pulsing in my neck: blood against gravity / hair unsheathed
by gravity. a confusion.   last weekend my sister led me up the side
of a mountain covered in snow.   the quaking aspen around us, she
explained,   were threads of a single organism – feathery shoots off one
ortet.   each in its own stage of adolescence.

when one of us trips, we strain the whole network under our feet.
I feel my mind worrying every root and rock.   *I'm sorry*, I say to
everyone inside it,   *I'm sorry I'm sorry*. to avoid closing my eyes
I'll light almost any memory on fire   and huddle around it.
how much of my skin is buried in the seams of this couch
how long will it last with this kind of pressure
                    my chakras burn an infinite hole into the fabric

ii. to understand the source material

inside the big hot hour

man: asleep
dog: long sleeping
the afternoon: languid and couched
my language: behind the curtain –

throbbing into the screen door
cicadas at its back, mites circling its haunches.
what to say to the overcast hour? this moment
twilight was conceived and

I birthed a great mountain of worries.
maybe the city doesn't function because some
people snore while others seize with anxiety.
who's to say that night will come?

is all I'm saying. if we haven't learned how
to talk to the ant, the sparrow, the lone black moth
who escaped into the kitchen yesterday, brimming
until my man cut him down with a dishtowel,

then who can understand us? is all I'm saying.
no, said someone. yes, said someone else.
they were looking at the same thing. it was the
hot hour. fish were sold. lawns were mowed.

I didn't understand the person typing this at the
kitchen table, biting her lower lip and staring
into the backyard. I crawled up next to her.
I patted her head anyway.

self-portrait as a baby

after the illustration "Portal Veins"
by Andreas Vesalius

if lifted from the body
        the belly's veins resemble
                        mangroves: equatorial thicket of spleen,
                wrought biliary root like sappy filigree –
        half water or blood,
half pillow-shaped sponge.

if I press my finger to a baby's
        pulse while she writhes and
                        pitches toward mother
            I am testing her like a compass,
        and all the iron in her body
        floods northward.

if eighteen years later
she is found maneuvering
        backwater tributaries
        without a paddle, call her
                brackish wanderer,

                        call her lost in blood.

                        if her age quintuples
                but her liver keeps its
                smooth sheen, say
        she has a lucky swamp inside.

    what do you carry?
    what do you carry?
my hands ask the baby's skin.

every vein ferrying something, every
child hurrying through the swamp
      with what will kill her
            tucked under her stomach.

                            arms wrapped around my own trunk
I cannot see through water this murky.

        look anyway, I tell her. the baby
          holds a mirror to my face.
             the silt thins
        at the bottom something gleams.

second attempt at going home

for Benoît

here are the deer tracks we kids called signs
of God – remember? here, our father's voice,
an olive oil lacquer over the dinner table:
this is what we believe, this is what we don't.

family is a kind of country, I think, like the one
we drew around the deer's hoof prints in the mud
of the dried-up creek in the woods behind our house.
we declared ourselves leaders, knowledge-keepers,

the way some humans will once they claim
a land as their own. my brother and I walk the
quiet streets of the country he calls home now,
and I confess to him that I've always felt in exile.

I read that Robert Hayden once said,
because no place is home, in a sense, everywhere
can be home. I tell my brother this and he smiles,
and the primroses open their moon faces toward

a statue of a leader on a rectangle of land called
a park. here we are, on a nearby bench, siblings
recalling the night sky from which we both came –
our mother. praise the woman who taught us how

to clean a bathtub well, how to sauté garlic and onions
like an invocation to the worship we'd do
in the kitchen. praise anyplace you
are well-fed. here is one way to go home:

find your brother, find a bench (any),
pull the yarn out of each other's throats until
your language finds its hooves again,
hear your common gallop over the land.

what if, more than place, it's about sound?

if it's movement that matters – places knit together
over time – vibrations – then I need to hear you
say what and where we are, no matter the answer,
and hear how many ways I can ask –

there is no word for (my mother's fear of everything that might touch me)

I want to be your mother, little dog,
or at least give you unbreakable bones.

I shield your eyes from road kill,
pry discarded gum from your jaw
when you tongue trash off the sidewalk.
the day you first tried to howl I finished the sound for you,
and now there are times I howl quietly to myself
in the closet, hoping the neighbors will assume it's you.

the truth is that I miss walking on all fours,
your sense of smell.
I look you in the eyes and see behind language.
I press the tiny pulse in your paw to my wrist,
the spot we are most related.

when my mother curved her hand around mine
to make letters, whenever I smelled her
smoldering panic, I wanted to bury the word
bone in her paw. we wrote *shelter*. we wrote
shell. as if trying to bark ever bucked a bite.

      but it could –
think about it: if you said the perfect thing
you would never have to say anything else.
all howls therefore lead to more howls.
sometimes we find it easier to love a dog than
to love other humans, and we worry this makes us
bad humans. actually, we are bad listeners.

what kind of word is *bad*, anyway?
I buried it in the backyard, little dog.
I left the space where it was
empty, for once.

I should have stayed in that silent moment,
but I pulled you into my lap and uttered fiercely.
I was just teaching you to keep existing.
I wonder if I am a bad mother.
are you listening?
I just want you to exist.

scholarship

to practice intense study. to research. to seek   again. to require confirmation,
a proof. to believe.   to believe in knowing because it can be said
again and again. the proving of a theorem.   now the corollary: to have learned axioms. to have
internalized them in one's axons. to know on a cellular level. to truth. to truthify. to embody theory.
not to be theoretical. to postulate. not to translate wherever possible. to hold lemmata in the hand:
leashed controllable.   to create the   boundaries of   to understand the source material
          the source text of
to become intimately familiar with the makings of   to understand   to stand
under law   proof in hand   to hypothesize codify declaim
          missing: complete allegiance to the hierarchy of epistemologies   lines of logic
               ob   je   ct   iv   it   y   as (a) knowable object(s).
          instead/and: slippage   the rush of senses   other lines etched around the eyes not
               logic-derived   the inconvenient soft casing of the brain.

I   taught control of the mind and its body   taught the mind belongs to the body   is to
be used in service of the body   and in this direction only enjoy scholarly work. I enjoy convincing
myself what is true   because it has been assembled before me   or I have deduced it   using
numbers and reason. I enjoy conjugating: placing the DNA of this epistemology   directly into my
cells   becoming this set of logics.   I climb   the hierarchy of epistemologies. here I do not
think about the softness of the brain   here I do not contemplate the science of neuroplasticity.
experience is unreliable/irreproducible therefore not of use   here   I simply receive. I have
been gifted with a task   trophied as someone else's proof of _____.   objectively, I
exist only in a Cartesian sense.

          you, knowledge – not producer – curator, have been given a set of postulates. you have
          been gifted have earned   have achieved financial resources with which to access the
          postulates. you have been entrusted. you have received a sort of trust funding. it is trusted
          that you will use it in the service of the State   which funds the University
          which does not discuss its source materials   which does not discuss its resources
          its human resources which is an environment for the storage of knowledge   which
          can be synthesized by the right person or persons   which is/are a set of working
          neurons which do not include said persons' bodies.   bodies of
          knowledge notwith

standing.   the ship(s) the scholars' bodies came in on. for what purpose. a purpose that
you have been invited to share   Dear Scholar.
the floating knowledge   knowledge of floating   the scholars at sea –

    he/she/it is blackboarded.
    he/she/it is presumably intelligent.
    he/she/it shines a light.
    he/she/it brings to bear.
    he/she/it hoists the load.
    he/she/it is calloused.
      is tired.
    he/she/it is unspecified.
    he/she/it is homeless.
    he/she/it has been erased.
      once loved erasers'
           hot rubber smell on the finger
           the way their dead skin rolls between the fingers and away
      once bled from the head
             loved

late spring

first thunderstorm of the year passes through
and afterward we lie awake listening to the woman across
the street curse her daughter: *i hope you die*, she screams,
the pavement steaming between words.

my ambivalence repels words –
we pass it back and forth, hands to hot hands,
but only one of us knows what we're handling.
you study me in the low light until I feel

like a foreign body. the basil plants feel
their thickening green paradoxical as beauty:
some beetle I've yet to see is working down
the leaves as soon as they unfurl.

the dog's splendid howl unfurls
when I turn off the hose and duck inside.
belonging means that someone is always
on one end of a leash.

even when he slips from his leash,
wet and muddy, shampoo foam flying,
dog never fully flees. it's the back-
yard chase he's after.

no one wants to know what comes after
someone's no longer after you. what I fear:
the curse of indifference, which is also trauma,
a hard mirror, nothing to pass through.

seventh attempt at going home

All weekend I've been waiting
to give our neighbors the box of

cookies & card we bought:
Congratulations on your citizenship!

but they don't answer to my knocks,
which means they've already learned

how to live in this country: with suspicion,
for who can say if it's a walking gun

or a tin man come to say how much money
you owe? My mother taught me to

arrange my face into wary lines,
to always ask what's in it for them.

Four centuries in, this place has offered us
only everything and nothing, which is

one of the arguments I've had for years
with a friend who immigrated, who pledges

she knows it like I can't, and I'm starting
to believe allegiance is closer than you'd think

to allege. As in, say one thing stands for another
long enough & soon you'll be convinced.

All weekend it rained, and I wondered
how much water the ground could

hold before chunks of earth started
melting off and flying into space,

soggy new mud-moons slinging
detritus & plastic scrap & human bone

into the antigravity. This year we accepted
a record low number of refugees in forty years.

The faster a body spins, the more
closely held its limbs, despite the signs

in front of every other townhouse that
proclaim all are welcome, that our lives

matter, no matter who we love, o si
hablamos español.   What's truer

is that when I pay taxes every year
I am complicit in un-homing people.

I'm still learning how to neighbor, and
if I'm honest, that means I'm still

learning how to be at home.
it's more than cookies, I know.

I know that water is neither created nor destroyed –
just melts & freezes & melts & freezes
                              & melts & melts & melts

When they finally emerged on Monday
I hurried out, unsure of what the congratulation

was for after all, so muttered happy holidays,
too. *Thank you!* said her bright face. *This is*

too much, but it wasn't. It wasn't anything
at all.

flash point

the people who were killed, the people who died
this week drifted from the branches and were swept into piles
into which the children threw themselves.
when the air gets colder
inevitably my thoughts turn to reproduction.
it is easier to slice a cell open than to divide it.
sometimes I imagine long-dead people reassembling / rehydrating / suddenly alive again.
for instance my grandfather.
as a child I feared spontaneous combustion. as an adult I constantly feel flammable.
my body is easy to crumple and light as a leaf.
the page offers fuel. my gathering anxiety
an aphrodisiac. could I teach my future children
how to be anything other than at war?
there is so much lying in wait on our stoops, behind the flowerpots,
according to our neurons.
I still jump back when the spider who lives on my front porch
scuttles away from my fingers reaching for the door handle.
she and I spend all day trying not to think about our deaths.
behind my sternum, a rope tightens.

long distance

driving in early winter to my love who lives three states away
sprays of blackbirds fling across the slough tucked into the curve of an exit ramp
where Pennsylvania gives way to Delaware of sheared cornfields, of farmhouses with their splintered
mouths opening to mudfields puddled with the palm of the sky, Lenape land, fields covered in defeated
stalks like small pyres pointing heavenward, clouds sworn to mundane iridescence.

time spells out the movement of all matter, but only matter.

to watch a day end: make your way through pink-skied country
how to hold the skeletons of poplars and power lines in the mind as they mark the miles – here
Maryland, here trees stripped of their flesh –

the road opens up the land and we ask
if we were meant to see it this way.

closer to heaven the geese are pointing southward and it seems a small miracle of organization, though
maybe every creature moves as diligently toward warmth as I do now. humans haven't yet learned how
not to kill ourselves a little each time we move.

now the moon is a bright coin, now a single planet hypnotizes, lantern-like, maybe more alive than this
one if we could set our hot feet on it. we call a thing lovely only after we have broken it.

confused animal I am, mesmerized by the goldening horizon, my movements as purposeful as a moth's
when viewed from a satellite that ribbons the earth for decades.
our heat-seeking will be the death of us – the same banality of a dozen moths' velvety bodies impaled on
my car's headlights

and at the end of these hours
there will be a glass of wine, some bread, the deep and satisfied stretch of my love's laughter over me.
the interstate behind me will not be filled in my mind with fur and smears of oil and entrails of unlucky
deer we leave in our wake.

for my father as a child it was the small magic of Christmas-lit homes that unstrung him down to his bright core; for my mother, the awakening in a scalding shower. we seem not to want for much, but oh, how even this much has taken! I think I love myself more than I love the land, and that may be my greatest grief one hundred years from now.

the presumptuousness of asking forgiveness in advance – of the reddening sky, of my grandchildren. the misguided thought that there is penance in a poem.
here is the Bay bridge, here the choppy Chesapeake waters, here the Virginia I love to love from behind glass, gulls dipping with each pulsing brake light predictable as a heartbeat.

love, pick something to sacrifice. by which I mean I want to be both human and an animal worthy of this speck of dust.

iii. yellow is the color of my wanting

haibun at Monticello

for Maura

through the woods   covered in draping green shadow   my cousin and I walk
        straight uphill   for a while not talking   just the distant
rush of cars   then we talk for a long time   about my new position as
Director of Diversity for the Department   and her dream to make White people Understand   (about
this place, its fathers   still alive   still doing their founding deeds)
we talk: where we'd like to live someday,   as if there's a country better than this
        you know how it goes   people think she's White until she tells them she's not/
won't align with that violence – not to mention   our brown fathers (brothers), our
        curly hair –   this story so old by now   the myth of it shows.

we cross wooden bridges over sodden patches   soaked in from all the rain
        mosquitoes humming up to our ankles   sweat   cicadas   creaking oak
        Virginia becoming rainforest before our eyes   money will do that to a place
drown it   make it something else   and when we get to the top of the hill   and cross the road
and pass a graveyard   we are at the Visitors' Center

Look, a man who thought he owned everything   is still being talked about on Sunday afternoons in
central Virginia: Look at his house, Look at his bed, Look at the view –
        and yes, slaves lived here, too.

we follow the tour guide along Mulberry Row   duck into a cool side wing of the big house and
there, small homage to Sally Hemings –
                what we learn: she might have stayed in France, where she'd have been free
                but that man, that man –

in this version sixteen-year-old Sally Hemings wins the
argument
takes up mending for the wealthy of Paris
saves enough to buy a small house for herself and
her young son. meets another man, who loves her.
she loves him. today no one knows her name other

than her great-great-great-great-grandchildren,
who speak fondly of their American ancestor
who wrenched herself away and mothered
alone for all those years in a foreign country.
nothing much else to say, besides
she baked a mean torte.

a story like this is why we are here –   we are not visitors

and where do we go? where do we go with it?

we turn away from the big house and   its lies
                                          trying to truth themselves greater

for a moment it's unclear how to pick up the path back down the mountain
               but the graveyard appears again   and we walk toward it

there are days

rage burns a hole through both hands.
I hear my descendants more loudly these
days, asking for answers. one use of a
uterus: anger machine, hot fist in my belly.

there will be a day I'll have to explain where I was,
which insects I sheltered, what I did with my money.
my chest a witness. in the documentary they forgave
the murderer – *something something religion*

but all I could pull up after were cramping sobs,
three-day panic – a kind of birth. in slow motion
my anxiety is actually grief. suddenly I can't
imagine a comfort other than salt water.

these days bumblebees have become
deified – sweet fumblers of fertility
bobbing around my tomato flowers.
no, I didn't ask to be angry. yes, I knew

it would settle along my bones and under
my spleen. yes, in those days medicine was
pollinated steam, dregs of tea, and begging
forgiveness of the future. my congested bloodbag.

I don't want to be a murderer but I still
pay taxes. now my palms are windows.
I plunge them into the bowl of my pelvis.
there are days I stir and stir and never cool.

My mother spent her life passing as white.
Discovering her secret changed my view of race — and myself.

I'd never seen   afraid.

years   waited for   my mother with the shocking.

In the records, my   entire family

            My sense   shattered.

                                    This was   a conversation I wanted to

have on the   fearful   identity.   I obtained

the state of   race   (colored).

Reluctantly, I   told no   children

the   most difficult secret I'd ever   skin

            silence   I tried to break. But

refusal.

deceived my racist   mystery
started sifting through   her life

clues   would help

this   intensified
truth   fiction.

of living in the   white   racist   reflection
                        close-knit   bigotry,

Was she afraid   ?
Did his racist   rain   ?
Or had   the lie   sat   ?
privilege was worth the price
shared   every day   with the paradox   called   the ambivalence.
mixed   with the trappings   a   retaliation
          imbued   with   a moral   color

rapt   with packages   concealed   serendipity

          welcome home   slave owners, enslaved women, and free people of color.

artifacts of daily wanting

I wonder where I'll be on that day.
it's faith that scares me, same as unbelief:
who am I to be right?

I envy the way you cup a palm, say
drink   as if all this – reproduction, vast
decadence of breathing – were my birthright.

I don't know tonight from any other.
an empty intersection's wan face,
I'm calculating so hard.

whatever can scratch the sidewalk
into giving up a little honey.
does time really remember us each day?

yesterday a boy with a faltering circuit
brain asked me if it would hurt, while
his mother inflated a bathroom with sobs.

it could be said that I ask for too much.
I'd just like to know if those are fireworks
in the garden or gunshots –

I'd like a fable with the smoke.
some cerated mornings trick me into
looking for the day's warm root.

I know I'll follow you toward
soft tea lights, a bed we keep making up,
but a wren in her brick nest doesn't ask

how eggs appeared under her belly.
one day these chicks' yawning beaks
will crown the exploding forsythia beneath.

remember permutations and combinations?
math terrifyingly endless. think of
all the things we could make:

my brain maps the garden
and the spread before us whispers
in a sunset empire voice –

slick poisonous sibilance I don't
dare blame on a snake, which
is just a miraculous tube of muscle.

I don't know how to twist with such
singularity toward the apple dangling
between us. I believe I'm ripe.

yes, it hurts, that's the moral of the story.
yellow is the color of my wanting.
I'll say to you, *here is honey – eat.*

Labor Day

we're in the pool with a handful of friends, old and new –
drove twenty miles out of town to dip into this blue pocket at the top
of a ninety-degree afternoon,
the friend who lives in the farmhouse greeting us with chilled wine,
a black puppy sleek and yapping beside her.   he adopted me, she smiles.

the dog tries putting his jaws around my wrist, and I yelp, like I read
you're supposed to do. he looks alarmed, drops me, apologizes with his eyes, his red tongue.   you're
good at that, says the friend, and I tell her I've been doing it
for months at home with my own dog.

except there are times I forget to yelp, get pulled into a sweet wrestle of (pony)tail and coiled knees on the ground,
like you're not supposed to do.   remember, you're a human.

we sip and eat the salsas and pies the friends have brought and laid on the table.
one woman says snakes are making homes in pool noodles now, and we peek into
the foam ends of ours, feign nervousness. but we admit it's ingenious.
imagine finding a perfectly human-shaped room in another creature's nest –
I'd slither in, too.

when the trees swallow the last of the sun we turn on the pool lights and become
bellies and limbs suspended in a green glowing rectangle.
coyotes start up a hollering racket not far away.
we feel loose, open-mouthed. it's hard work remembering to be human,
and that's what we're here to celebrate today, with chlorine & grill
at the edge of a wild we crave.

clockmelt

over acid-bitten glaciers, in oils in the style of

Dalí, set in the time of global warming –

you can imagine it, can't you? plastic

drums of earth-blood rolling into the open

mouth of the ocean while a continent away moon

after moon reels by & autumn seedling hearts

thrum beneath the window, every month a new river

of blood to measure the distance from here to

one sort of mothering, the race for a vaccine an ultra-

marathon through briared wilderness as friend

after friend around me splits herself

to usher future melodies, meconium-slick.

I'm unlearning to tell time by the furling of

leaves, by the return of cool air like a prodigal

cousin – when she saunters in, mink to

the floor, smelling of sage & wood smoke,

after the world has spun and warmed

record-breakingly, I'm a little shocked she's made

the journey yet again. I fall asleep to a familiar

rhythm, circadian blues that for months

rocked me in wordless silence while I searched

my throat for poems, and now that it's the season

of birds aiming south & finding my love's

palm & crickets modulating their

key & days crisping up around the

edges I decide I can trust this dance after all.

through my sci-fi dystopian haze

the warble of B.B. King's harmonica scalloped

this morning into halves, the contours of my

fatigue a brightly weaving bivalve – faith is the

knowledge that this precise loneliness will

circle back around at regular intervals

divinable only by the rain that starts at midnight.

in a midnight assemblé on my retinas, the future

& irredeemable past blaze in and out of focus

like this year's three hundred wildfires – controlled only

by the winds. my digital presence can't touch this, but

my adamant capillaries can, pulsing over and

over under my fingerprints under the sheets

to the beat of miniature spinach roots feeling

through compost in the raised bed twenty

feet below to the beat of magma heaving

subterranean waves two thousand miles

below that, which is the kind of timing

I have to believe in if I want to make it

out of here with my living intact. the

second hand slides down the flowering cactus

next to the sink in the last shards of twilight

as I go to work remaking our bodies daily with

sweet carbohydrate & pattern, unfathomable

two-legged waste rushing us toward an end.

mother, I want to say, teach me again

how to tell time.

haibun in the year of return

the ocean   I cried drunkenly   *is my mother*

you tipped your head   sea spray slipped into your throat

I wanted to walk into the high tide –   not to die, exactly,

     but to feel better

               the aftershocks of becoming

oscillating   in the dark century   – –

               two months later

on another coast, we gorge on salted shrimp and crab

legs   I hate myself for judging the mom way

all the mothers clasp their toddlers' fingers with wet wipes

and twist   we go home where all

we want to do is drink water after water

in Ghana I saw sheets of sardines spread out to dry

along the road like metal earth shields deflecting

the equatorial light –   reminded me of my mother

protecting us from ourselves   at the end of the

dust road, waving with fingers the size of continents for

me to keep walking, that she'd meet me on the other –

I remember you kept losing a shoe to the water

as she chased us up the beach, back toward the

safety net of palms   and as we scuttled you

murmured nauseously,

                              do you love me? are

you sure?

                    do you remember?

                                        I ask, my hands

still smelling like Old Bay and shrimp shells, but

you shake your head no.

                         a better question would be,

how?   though nothing I summon would explain the

sequence of events nor fully recollect the ships,

the planes, all the near-death twisted from our finger-

tips before being released from mother's grip.

I can't fathom it   I mean I cannot

plumb this kind of depth   I'm six feet under

the surface and still not sure

                    what my mother means.

stranded octopus syndrome

I don't feel the way I'm supposed to on vacation.
suggestion: *relax*
suggestion: *chill*
    i.e., cool the mind / stop the vibration

which generates heat / look at the ocean now—

of possibilities, and I said that's exactly what scares me.

my lover said, the ocean is supposed to make you think

the foam's intensity,   even from the vacation cottage window,
even with the sheen   of rain on top.   *suppose* is part of the problem, too close

to *pose*   which is to posture   perhaps imposter   and I have   a hard time faking it.
I used to think the cure was   lover, chocolate cake, a patchwork passport. as if
I were diseased.
    of course I enjoy   wine and the fancy   almonds   we brought, but Big Water's main effect is

to remind me that I'm a   part of it,   while apart from
it, same as I am   everything else.   I worry that the real me is somewhere under those waves, so in my brain

the heat cranks up. lonely people tend to take hotter showers,   the way my anxiety bundles me up, binds   me in a vise, a well-meaning
octopus too scared to
return to the ocean from where it came.

as if it were   not   a slippery missive sent directly from the deep.

53

eleventh attempt at going home

after Jenny Xie

smell of city: exhaust pipes & overripe mango crammed into a butcher's shop.
I've been told I'm never satisfied.

days I've slept in hammocks surrounded by unknown flora.
days I've wandered the Old City, sun throwing itself from the white walls onto my skin.
      whatever that violent light releases in me dancing itself into exhaustion.

*

smell of country (which?): equal parts wild onion, honeysuckle, & cow dung.
my privilege is that I rely on buses for time travel, can stare out a greasy window &
      directly into the past.

nights I've been unable to describe the contours of my interior.
the power goes, the water shuts off – even my sweat has awoken, parched.
price of my desire: white coin of the moon, lavender-drenched bed sheets looking
      for a piece of sleep, & my lover's peace.

*

smell of mountain: wood smoke folded into needling pine, spring mud, burnt tortilla.
in every face I look for resemblance.

an old story – somewhere in this market is a long-lost quarter-sister or half-cousin.
      somewhere here is the rest of me.

*

smell of sea: fish fried with lime, desiccating seaweed, great salt lick on the tongue
        of this continent.

I hear waves & jet engines gunning skyward.
the salt water in me rises to meet the eye of the sea.

what does it mean that I feel this craving under my diaphragm?

*

something arrives on my shores every time I get there:
what history has saved for me in this impossible leaving –

this is the consequence of several centuries' scattering and/or
        a dissolution of my own borders, slow and deliberate as a drum.

*

bellyful of plantains and rice, passport pressed between palms,
in customs I declare my shadow self & the two-hundred-year-old missing link.

officials don't know what to do with me.   are you coming or going? they ask

        I tell them I don't know yet.

wish you were here

I want to try to tell you
about how lucid the water
was that day, how purposeful
the sun, how the wind
snapped a linen sheet open-
mouthed as a sail over
the railing at the end of
the pier –   I wrote,

wish you were here

and meant it only
halfway through,

the line breaking off
and twisting at *you*,
my bare feet pointing
southward,
the soft and hard ocean
mewling so close I could
see the back of her
turquoise eye.

no one else can stand
in exactly the spot where
I'm standing, and
it's taken three decades' walking
to say I love you
to the inevitability of my solitude.

next to me
a man was coaxing his camera
into capturing this, like trying
to huddle fish together, their
silver bodies knives
slipping between his fingers.

we are always approximating –
see how the light changes just
before the shutter fires. I meant
to tell you   I want to say   that
this is as close
as we're going to get:

I love.   wish you.

a jellyfish is pulsing over
white sand six feet below my soles,
the photographer is angling to my right,
on my left a dark streak of coral,
and above my head a pelican, empty-
beaked, glints against a single cloud.

no one will ever be here again.
the line is scalloped and fleshy,
tastes of salt-rock. I suck it dry.

iv. I am not absent, as never before –

(driftwood)

—we are witnessing a great age	◊Love set sail centuries ago and I can still feel: 1) wind at my soles 2) salt spray on my teeth	we made our (waterlogged) bed, now	protects & strengthens skin's moisture barrier up to 48 hours*

I remember seeing
the body of a sparrow
in the parking lot of the
narrow building where
I did research one year
	capsaicin burn me
	
	brighter / brighter
	
	      sharpen my
	song / along tongue-
	blade / solar flare me
	closer to
		
		*lie your head on
		my bound wrists*
			...wet & ringing
			I emerge from water
			    onto land
			that has always known
			my name—

I bow to sassafras
cattail / fox darting
in front of my
headlights /
petrochemical dawn
/ the marsh fog
intoxicating almost to
orgasm…
	*two suns later I'm
	sweating ceramides and
	safflower oil
	
	snapping my fingers
	
	counting backward◊
		particleboard,
		fluorescence,
		neonicotinoids:
		
		*this, too, is our
		inheritance.*
			I don't want
			   don't want
			   don't—

I went to the North

for Tété-Michel Kpomassie

the wish for another side of life
starts with simple subtraction: to never again
see a snake. to never wrestle with the demands
of powerful men, ending belly-up.

> *As soon as they saw me, all talking stopped*
> *and the children were so afraid, some started weeping.*

silence stirs mystery deeper: puddle to ocean,
ocean to antimatter. dredging the depth, you see yourself,
decades ago, on a hot beach, feel again your surprise at
releasing the branch, swift breathlessness of the fall.

> *I started a journey of discovery*
> *only to find that I was being discovered.*

you learn that the snow hides ice, which often
hides water, a nearly-frozen sea in which –
yes, there are living fish! there is a world
that makes sense only in its own tongue.

> *Oh, where is that paradise?*
> *It is my country, yes.*

after you dreamt in that language
after you made brothers
after you decided to return home
then this place became of you.

Then I was happy because
I really conquered my freedom.

it's obvious now, on the way back to Africa,
leaning over the railing as the ship bites through waves,
the secret of the seagull – it's her submission
to the wind that frees her.

Ode to smoked salmon jerky

Ode to the moment, in the car,
on the luscious, drenched coast of Oregon,
I bit into it for the first time –

Ode to the Chinook people whose land,
roughly snatched, was home to this fish long
before it was home to the strip mall
parking lot next to Barnacle Bill's, which
is my current asphalted heaven –

Ode to their name, which they gave this
particular species of coldwater fish,
thick pink flesh ribbed with good
fat, the kind bottled into vitamins
and sold to people who spend too
much time in parking lots and the dim
sadness of buildings –

Ode to the way each molecule, simple or
complex, fits into this miraculous Earth –
from near-freezing grows a medicinal lipid
that eases the gears of our loneliest
cerebra, gets us closer to the fish cousins
who know to swim against the current
only when it's life or death –

Ode to the sweet, sticky glaze that for an hour
or two smoked me out of that day's upstream
fight with myself, and into the thanking ring
of fins and hands, into the holy river
where land and sea beings meet –

Ode to the way I have looked at every
image of a salmon since then with
new reverence, as evidence of order
that my whirring brain, my nearsighted
eyes, were not made to understand –

the junkyard galaxy knocks

for a long hour my dog sits, head cocked
as a ready hand, stares toward the plum-
drenched window where nothing is visible

to me but a neighbor's TV pulse of blue
light. I wonder what he sees beyond –
or in – the pane. when I first rented

this place with its sweeping ceiling of
exposed beams, I asked the landlady
who'd lived here before, last century,

and it was blind men & women workers
for a local factory. then again, you don't know
what you can't see. my dog blinks at the dark,

swivels ears toward the black hole of glass.
sometimes the ceiling drops nubs of carbonized
wood like asteroids onto my white sofa. I pluck

them off carefully. I have a bouquet of
comet shards flung from my roof, but who
brings space debris indoors? I start to believe

it's whoever's in the window, and yes,
there are times the other windows howl
a loose-jointed chorus of clattering thwacks,

sounding both fragile and like a fist
punching the glass. I tell my lover over
the wind, *if I ever wake up as a dog*

you'll know it's me. keep the dog with you
if I do. and how will he see that it's me,
he wants to know. I say,

just look. a window is a portal –
somewhere in space-time there are animals who
see what we can't conjure even in sleep.

who decides where a roof ends
and the junkyard galaxy begins –
when I say *hello love* and he peers under

the blinds of my eyelashes, is what he sees
what I think he sees? when I say *ability*
sometimes I mean a spot in the spherical,

gaseous planet of ability. I blink into
myself, trying to unsmudge the fenestra.
who's there? I ask my dog. *who's there?*

the house

not-writing feels like a form of self-
effacement, so for months now I've kept
mum – silent as I signed the mortgage,
as I donned the dress, silent as I
performed my privileges, more gent-
ry on fire than gentrified, more gent-
eel than gentle. when I don't know
what to do it's best to forget that
I'm doing anyway.
when I decide to write again I'll say,
          uncover your eyes, little
monkey, see the evil and step inside:
this, too, is your house.

IPCC says I'm a destroyer
Republicans say I'm crying
wolf, like acid snowflakes sub-
limating the permafrost into flame-
tongues. if my breath is smoke
and my eyes are mirrors
who's to say I'm anything but
a pretty distraction?

erasure of a letter to the current homeowners:

Dear   moment   driving through   a double take.
I grew up   twenty years ago.
                I never thought   the reason   I'm starting
        poetry   is   cultural preservation,
new   sense of rootedness.

at twilight on the eve
everything   at first sight was confirmed.
The street   history with deep roots
this   house   feels like an ancestor.
ownership of this   legacy   deserves care.
The   perfect   sweet   space to run.
We are enamored.

Twenty years ago I never*
It's funny how life works.
After   we approached,
"Does this feel like coming home?"

Thank you for considering us.

*NB: the hubris of believing one could choose one's place & people / not the other way around

I'd rather pretend I'm a representation
of the earth than enact my actual earthness:

      inside the house we put:
dream of babies   (human, dog)
wineglasses   alarm system   plant-
based bathroom cleanser
books
      books   books
seven-foot sunflower sculpture made of copper roofing scraps my love once drove from central Virginia
to Philly, as a way to celebrate my birth.

      outside the house we put:
a variety of flowers for the pollinators
dog's extra water bowl   rocking chairs
      (white picket fence was already there)
citronella candles   raised beds for next year's
      tomatoes zucchini lettuce & thyme
which we plan to share with the neighbors
never mind this year our zucchini putrefied from the
inside, shriveling to dead-gray overnight
– invasive mycosis, said my dad – *since when*
did we let a little rot keep us from rooting anyway

view from the front porch
with biological anthropology in the background:

the performance of living well is an intrinsic
aspect of living well. predating social media,
this ability to meta-experience one's own
experience is an inherent function of the human brain,
arising from its abundant cortical matter;
because of this divergence from other primate species
we then judge both our experience
and our meta-experience. authenticity
is a measure of the extent to which we are able to
pretend our performance is nonexistent – our ability
to perform non-performing. the delta between
the people we imagine we're becoming and
the people we are, as evidenced by our experiences,
becomes a source of anxiety. every day people
drown trying to cross the threads of alluvium,
which can be unexpectedly deep long before the
receiving ocean comes into view.

inspection:

stainless steel appliances, light fixtures
tasteful in their modernity, stucco walls
of a grandparent's home, functioning fireplace,
painted radiators, restored hardwood floors.
stale goldfish crackers in the crawlspace
behind the closet. doorknob wobbly. leaky
shower head.
      in the cellar, white mold. a whole beam
      insufficiently supported – yawn that won't
      close under the dining room.
            and the steps to the bulkhead storm door: hopping
            with those big-kneed crickets that love the dark
            and a pile of slugs, rippling with slime.

economies of legacy:

through an online search we find out the house was built by a certain Mr. R. B_____ in 1931,

that the B_____ family lived in it for eighty-plus years before an architect-realtor couple

cleared the termites and installed contemporary lighting and a butcher-block island;

that the B_____ family still lives in town.

in fact, one descendant is fighting for fair housing policy.

I grew up in this town, then moved away.

my husband is from one hour south.

this neighborhood had a certain name when it was full of Black professional families,

but it got another name when those families had to leave.   (Economics.)

my husband loves his hometown, but I think it's too small a place.

some in human resources would call us Black professionals because we have ample melanin and degrees.
  (Scholarship.)

where there are limited resources we have to think carefully about the use of those resources / the
  transfer of wealth.   (Economics.)

culture is a kind of resource.

the people who moved into the neighborhood when its first families moved out are called White.
no, those families weren't the first.

before the Black professionals there were Monacan families, I think.

this was the town of Monasukapanough.

before them – I don't know.

nowadays in this town, culture = very small small plates at a restaurant with exposed brick.

this is mostly a rich x White way of thinking, and it's in my brain.

this is why I can't live in a small place.

Economics is about the maximization of wealth x color, which = smaller and smaller, attractively
  presented farm-to-table morsels.

one way to measure the price of a home: expensive, but to whom.

if I peel back layers and expose the brick, then the mortar between, then the hands that laid those bricks
  (Scholarship),

then I have to ask, at least, how do you want to be called?

I have to ask, at most, who is caring for the land on which sit
the neighborhood, the farms, the tables, and the house?

if we refuse *husband* and *wife*
if we carve out spaces wide enough for each of our whole selves
our loved ones   and those we will love
if we include in the above category anyone who crosses the threshold
if we include grandfather house himself
if we allow even what we find in dank corners
if we siphon underground water out of stone-filled air
and send it to the roots of pepper and basil along the wall
if we use less each year
if we leave offerings for sentinel tree, nonagenarian stairwell
if we keep all our names
if we teach our children this cumulative song
if, in purchasing the title, we can become unentitled,
        wake up each day with the same grateful shock
        of breaking lake water with a face
if we call this *home* and approach it at dusk –

I'm not from here / but twenty years ago / I grew up here – I stopped not-writing
I left and came back / I wake up each day with / a lake water love / from south of here – maybe this is as
close / as I'll get: the questions / of my earthness held
by these gentle walls / and shore-arms / before seeping back
into the big water of living –

found

the black moth flickering in and out   of my eyefield
the wind blowing   sunlight sideways   in shards
the fan   sashaying its   small-hipped dwindle
the body (mine) switching shoulder blade over spine
not to let   the moth   caress my face, for

the wordless unluck of it, as I believe – in
the moment I   feel nothing   touching me –
the flickering shards,   dwindling sashay,
the hypnosis of midday. someone is humming nearby,
not a song so much   as a thread of notes,

the air peppered hot with them. I'm one of
the lucky ones, because   I freeze seeing
the black   wings scattering beams all through
the flaring curtain   of my sight – then it turns, a
          knot buried inside me   flying open.

the someone humming has stopped.
the old man a few seats down sighs, uncrosses
the arms.   I think of the sea this morning, along
the highway, as it slowly rose up from the retreat of
not night, but something deeper –

the diaspora of notes, I think, that is pulling me to
the plane, to the page, to these hands' flutter in
the brinking moment. unlikely, lucky sunlight.
the beams scatter and narrow.   I am
          not absent, as never before –

overlap

in the tea shop: smell of old hookah clings to us
friends sighing about ex-spouses(' exes),
who seem to hang in the air, on our arms and faces, too.

I'm listening – no, I'm thinking
about how the dance of closing
and opening the distance between us is a drama that
sears down to the bones' thin lining, tries to
scrape the white desert beneath shiny periosteum.
even when a person leaves, however they leave,
they're attached to the other forever – I mean we even
alter the shape of each other's bodies, says my friend,
whose allergies are worse now than they've ever been.

there's something here about how getting close
means looking your death in the face –

I don't mean your dying, I mean the one you love,
worse because it's imaginable.
my grandmother can tell you how it feels,
her mattress can tell you the sobs it cradled,
her apartment measures my grandmother's feelings

by how many boxes are still unpacked, by the weighty
exhalation of bubble-wrapped paintings
leaning against the wall.

that's a kind of death, isn't it, the refusal to be
completely here, open-eyed? and are we all a little
dead the way we glance away from headlines
and shudder the radio off before blood begins
to leak onto the kitchen counter freshly wiped,
still smelling of lemon?

I want to be close, in the
thick mess of us, but my anxiety wants me straight-
up and clean, all unbroken lines and corners
tucked in. maybe I meant trauma, not drama.
there's something here about heaviness
– the look of my mortality and yours,
constant and unblinking, the muscles behind my eyes
tense from averting my gaze
                         (if I do this long enough
I'll grow a different kind of pain).

                                        this morning I was shocked
                    to walk into my favorite coffee shop
                    and find flowers over all the tables, memorial
                    to its co-founder, who died, I found out a few
                    minutes later, eight days ago, thirty-four years old,
                    survived by his wife and young son,
                                        and I think
                    what bothers me is the word *survived*. it's just too
                    early to say.

my grandmother has fallen three times now –
there are pins holding her hip together
she wants to walk again but she doesn't:
she says she misses him, and it covers her
like a great blanket of fog – she remembers less
these days – I remind her to look up, look ahead,

but we both know these are just distractions –
the bigger issue is that he is dead. lead-weight
word, sunk in the throat, threatening to pin
down the tongue,   word as toll across the
Styx, word that sticks, unyielding, refuses
to loosen but will loosen teeth, chip and
worry them right out a mouth   – mine –
to say it too much.

now that I see his face on the obituary-flyer
in the coffee shop window I remember
the few times he rang up my single-source
eye-opener, cup of beans to laser-focus
me, tunnel-visioned, ahead.
I remember his smile,
          calm smile of a person who has
done a thing he set out to do, which is make
a space that brings people elbows-close,
a place where, even if lost in screens,
we notice how our bodies breathe
together, one caffeinated collective –

me + the man next to me who laughs softly
at moving images on his phone
+ the grayed woman in ill-fitting jeans
who opens a Bible while she waits
+ finally my love, who comes to spend
a moment of the workday with me.

there's something here about not
looking away, no matter how close
you get to the surface of my bones
enhanced by vitamin D supplements
but still breakable, even by you.

come on, many-faced marriages, pour our
feelings into my cup. knowing how not to
break is less important than looking
every word in the face.

protection spell

I'm oiled and waxing gibbous in the hallway mirror
like the belly of the sky breath-stacking on its way
to an early morning snowfall.
I still wait on nights like these the way a child does –
excitable and straining against probabilities.
so much about me has never grown up, as in,
I'd be lying if I said mean strangers on the Internet don't bother me.
Against sticks or stones or shards of letters, I hold my breath as I
grow out, rely on rituals from centuries ago to keep what's in me
on track: sign of the cross, ginger crushed between my teeth,
amethyst held in my hollow of neck. I'm collecting ways
to keep the evil eye above the clouds closed –
the snow sizzles as it hits the fractious embers of
the great iris – parting the airstreams, my language is
a force of nature.

third attempt at going home

if not rejection of the commodification of my identity
                        if not neither here nor there
          if not subject to crosswinds and climate change
if not a loose net of stories
                                        if not always something there to remind me
if not a sonata   if not a trinity   if not holy
                    if not a three-legged dog
          if not the taste of bread
if not a manifestation of ego
                        if not a shadowy projection
if not a wild eel   if not electrifying and difficult to hold
          if not an intergenerational rope of muscle
if not the negative of what surrounds it
                    if not black and white   if not covered in blood
if not a site of conscience
          if not a sight of relief
          if not a citation in the bibliography of self
                                                  if not requiring me
if not required for my sins of self
          if not about ownership   if not about the reappearance of names
if not about languaging existence onto land   if not a survival mechanism
          if not that which keeps a body in motion
                        if not an antidote to stagnation (death)
          if not a bright dream burning as we run toward it
if not flammable as my hair   if not made of matchsticks and sugar cubes
          if not an unreadable map to an empty room
          if not a place to set everything down, to lay it out, to finally say what we are,
                    once and for all,
                        then I don't know what.

never have I ever

Mother's Day I'm at work, where the hospital ward is thick with babies.
I enter room after room to look into their eyes – long-awaited or unexpected guests,
the babies stare at me, solemn and decisive: the next links in a chain of desire older
than any of us can imagine. later that day I order a hands-free breast pump,
giddy with the thought of making myself into food. I love land so much I become it.
I want more so badly I'll make it from my own body.

behind the final door, an operating room,
parents beaming under heat lamps –
the abundance of twins – my own baby swelling
against my scrubs as I congratulate them.

never have I ever wanted so much – eating ice cream at any hour, crying over the chorus
of spring peepers Dopplering through the passenger window, my whole body a horde of
seventeen-year cicadas wrestling their way up from the dirt. I said I wouldn't want so much the wiser I
got, but Earth, forgive me: I got drunk on thick-knotted blackberry
rising from the humid flank of this land, breathed a dream of ancient honeysuckle and
crabapple, woke in a wetland clutching cattail & throating a swallow's nesting song –

this is the Day my mother has made   today I walk into room after room
          today I tell the babies: never have I ever known a way to be   that wasn't
velvety white on the tongue   sweet salt & fat   letters curdled in the mouth,
rising from amniotic foam   at the moment of the first shout !

Notes

In "there are days," the documentary film referenced is *Emanuel*, which is about the 2015 white supremacist massacre of nine people at Emanuel African Methodist Episcopal Church in Charleston, South Carolina.

"eleventh attempt at going home" is after multiple poems from *Eye Level*, by Jenny Xie.

"My mother spent her life passing as white. Discovering her secret changed my view of race — and myself." is an erasure of an article by the same name, written by Gail Lukasik (*Washington Post*, Nov. 20, 2017).

In 'I went to the North,' italicized lines are direct quotes from a video interview with Tété-Michel Kpomassie entitled "An African boy's remarkable odyssey to the Arctic," available from the BBC: https://www.bbc.com/news/av/stories-48107317/an-african-boy-s-remarkable-odyssey-to-the-arctic.

In "the house," IPCC is an acronym for the Intergovernmental Panel on Climate Change.

In "third attempt at going home," the line "always something there to remind me" is the title of a song by Naked Eyes.

Acknowledgments

Immense gratitude for the following journals, in which versions of these poems first appeared:

"After emailing a copy of Audre Lorde's essay / 'The Uses of the Erotic' to a friend" and "second attempt at going home" in *Jet Fuel Review*.

"My head is full of powers," "inside the big hot hour," and "Labor Day" in *Shenandoah*.

"the forest fire of family trees," "there are days," and "haibun in the year of return" in *The Boiler*.

"fourteenth attempt at going home," "late spring," and "the junkyard galaxy knocks" in *Blackbird*.

"lullaby" in *American Poetry Review*.

"scholarship" and sections from "the house" in *Virginia Quarterly Review*.

"seventh attempt at going home" in *Hampden-Sydney Poetry Review*.

"flash point" in *The Shallow Ends*.

"long distance" in *Wildness*.

"haibun at Monticello" and "third attempt at going home" in *Under a Warm Green Linden*.

"artifacts of daily wanting" in *Empty Mirror*.

"clockmelt" in *EcoTheo Review*.

"eleventh attempt at going home" in *Scalawag*.

"wish you were here" and "(driftwood)" in *Four Way Review*.

"Ode to smoked salmon jerky" in *River Mouth Review*.

"found" in *Rabbit Catastrophe*.

Deep appreciation to the editors of the following anthologies, in which these poems also appeared:

"haibun in the place of sleep" in *What Tells You Ripeness* (Pangyrus, 2021).

"self-portrait as a baby" in *Imagining Vesalius: An Ekphrastic, Scholarly, and Literary Celebration of the 1543* De Humani Corporis Fabrica *of Andreas Vesalius* (UCSF Medical Humanities Press, 2020).

"there is no word for (my mother's fear of everything that might touch me)" in *The Familiar Wild* (Sundress Publications, 2020).

"long distance" in *Wildness Omnibus, 2015 - 2019* (Platypus Press, 2019).

"the junkyard galaxy knocks" in *Best American Poetry 2022* (Scribner, 2022).

"never have I ever" in *The Southern Poetry Anthology, Volume IX: Virginia* (Texas Review Press, 2022).

Abundant gratitude for the writings of Audre Lorde, Jenny Xie, Aracelis Girmay, and so many others whose work directly or indirectly inspired these poems.

To Sebastián Páramo, Will Evans, and the entire Deep Vellum team: it has been an honor to make this book with you. Ginger Huebner, thank you for painting my words – may our ekphrastic collaboration keep singing through the coming years.

To my Philly poets circle – Shevaun Brannigan, Raena Shirali, Tim Lynch, Nomi Stone, Daniel Brian Jones, & Alan Beyersdorf – thank you for thinking about many of these poems with me. To the Charlottesville poets who provided aesthetic advice in the final stages of this book's journey – Valencia Robin and Aran Donovan – thank you for your keen eyes and honesty. To Ben Martin and to Brian Teare – thank you for our ongoing discourse and work on the healing powers of language. Gratitude to the Virginia Center for the Creative Arts for providing time and space to write or revise many of these poems.

To my loves and catalysts – Justin Reid, Jeannette Mathieu, Benoît Mathieu, Watts, Maggie Guggenheimer, garden seedlings, Grandma Louise, Grandpa Owen, Maura Mathieu, Miranda Bennett, Chinook salmon, Mom, Dad, Sheba, Raja, wetlands, Lilia Fuquen, Celeste O'Brien, bumblebees, Chesapeake Bay, neighbors, patients, aspen(s), sardines and other small fish, Grandfather House, spiders, celestial bodies, crickets, unnamed photographer, wrens, snakes, land, unnamed trees, mothers, (the mother of mothers) the ocean, & my dear daughter – this book is made of you.

IRÈNE P. MATHIEU (she/her) is an academic pediatrician, writer, and public health researcher. She is author of *Grand Marronage* (Switchback Books, 2019), which won Editor's Choice for the Gatewood Prize and runner-up for the Cave Canem/Northwestern Prize; *orogeny* (Trembling Pillow Press, 2017), which won the Bob Kaufman Book Prize; and *the galaxy of origins* (dancing girl press & studio, 2014). Her poems have appeared in *American Poetry Review*, *Narrative*, *Boston Review*, *Southern Humanities Review*, *Los Angeles Review*, *Callaloo*, *Foundry*, *TriQuarterly*, and elsewhere. Irène has received fellowships from the Fulbright Foundation, Callaloo Creative Writing Workshop, and the Virginia Center for the Creative Arts. Irène is an assistant professor of pediatrics and assistant co-director of the Program in Health Humanities at the University of Virginia. For more information please visit irenemathieu.com.

CPSIA information can be obtained
at www.ICGtesting.com
Printed in the USA
JSHW050202270423
40854JS00001B/1

9 781646 052660